I WANT TO BE A
NURSE

By Joanna Brundle

BookLife
PUBLISHING

©2020
BookLife Publishing Ltd.
King's Lynn
Norfolk PE30 4LS

A catalogue record for this book is available from the British Library.

ISBN: 978-1-78637-945-0

Written by:
Joanna Brundle

Edited by:
William Anthony

Designed by:
Lydia Williams

All facts, statistics, web addresses and URLs in this book were verified as valid and accurate at time of writing. No responsibility for any changes to external websites or references can be accepted by either the author or publisher.

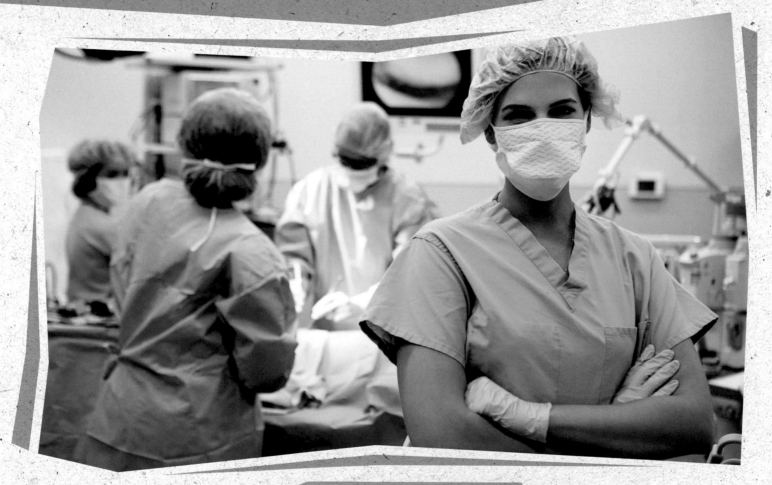

PHOTO CREDITS:

Images are courtesy of Shutterstock.com.
With thanks to Getty Images, Thinkstock Photo and iStockphoto.
Front Cover – AJR_photo, arka38, vectorchef, Africa Studio, VikiVector, Africa Studio, Vova Shevchuk, Wstockstudio, photo_jeongh.
2 – Monkey Business Images. 3 – Monkey Business Images. 4 – Alfazet Chronicles , michaeljung. 5 – michaeljung. 6 – michaeljung.
7 – alexkatkov. 8 – ChameleonsEye. 9 – goodluz, Goldsithney. 10 – wavebreakmedia. 11 – Monkey Business Images, Monkey Business Images.
12&13 – EPSTOCK, NineBall Foto. 14 – Maridav, XiXinXing. 15 – Laura v.d. Broek. 16&17 – sumire8, Henrik Dolle, Seasontime, AVAVA, catshila,
Lubos Chlubny. 18 – Monkey Business Images. 19 – DGLimages. 20 – Adam Jan Figel. 21 – SRIMES RATTANACHAI.
22&23 – Yusnizam Yusof, JPC-PROD. Vectors throughout: Africa Studio, ArdeaA.

CONTENTS

Words that look like <u>this</u> can be found in the glossary on page 24.

HELLO, I'M NOAH

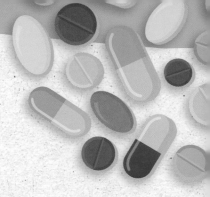

Hello, I'm Noah! When I grow up, I want to be a nurse. You could be one too! Let's find out what this job will be like.

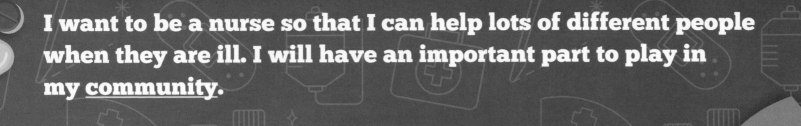

I want to be a nurse so that I can help lots of different people when they are ill. I will have an important part to play in my <u>community</u>.

People all over the world get poorly, so nurses are needed everywhere.

WHAT WILL I DO?

I will carry out doctors' instructions, giving <u>patients</u> any <u>treatments</u> or medicine that they need. I will also check people's <u>temperature</u> and <u>blood pressure</u>, give injections and treat injuries.

This nurse is checking someone's pulse (how many times the heart beats in one minute).

I may run special sessions at a health centre, looking after new babies or patients with conditions such as <u>asthma</u>. I will tell patients about how to live a healthy lifestyle.

Fresh fruit and vegetables and lots of exercise help to keep us healthy.

HOW WILL I HELP PEOPLE?

There are nurses to help everyone, from elderly patients to tiny, newborn babies.

I will look after and treat patients with all sorts of health conditions. I will care for them while they recover from illnesses, operations or accidents.

It can be upsetting and frustrating to be poorly, so I will help patients by being kind and explaining things clearly. I will help them to stay as healthy as possible.

WHERE WILL I WORK?

I might work in a health centre. This is where patients usually come if they are feeling unwell. Nurses, doctors and other healthcare workers all work together at a health centre.

Some nurses work in care homes for the elderly.

This is a theatre nurse. Theatre nurses help with operations.

I might become a hospital nurse. A hospital is separated into different parts that look after patients with different needs. I might work on a children's <u>ward</u>, or a ward for elderly people.

LET'S LOOK AROUND
A HOSPITAL WARD

Hospital beds can move up or down. The beds are on wheels so they can be moved easily.

NO SMOKING

NO SMOKING

Each bed has a call bell. The patient presses it to call a nurse.

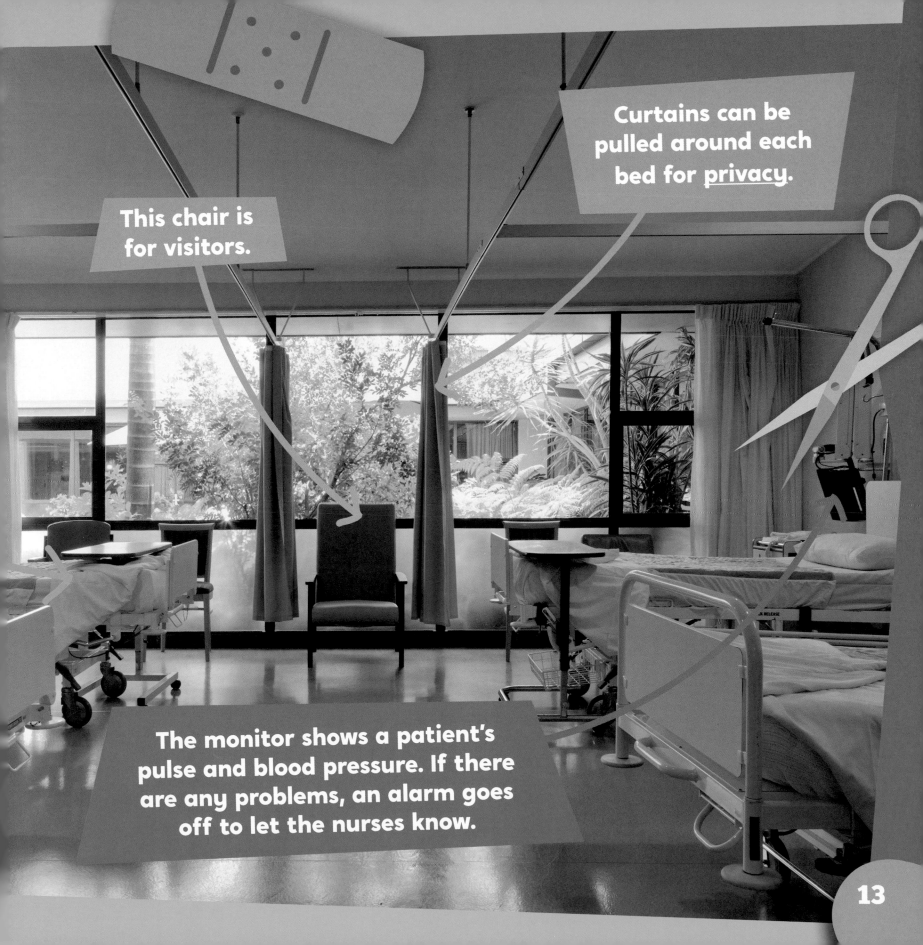

Curtains can be pulled around each bed for <u>privacy</u>.

This chair is for visitors.

The monitor shows a patient's pulse and blood pressure. If there are any problems, an alarm goes off to let the nurses know.

13

WHAT WILL I WEAR?

I will wear a tunic and trousers, or scrubs. Scrubs are comfortable, loose-fitting shirts and trousers. They are usually blue, green or white.

Scrubs

Nurses who work with children may wear brightly coloured scrubs, printed with fun designs.

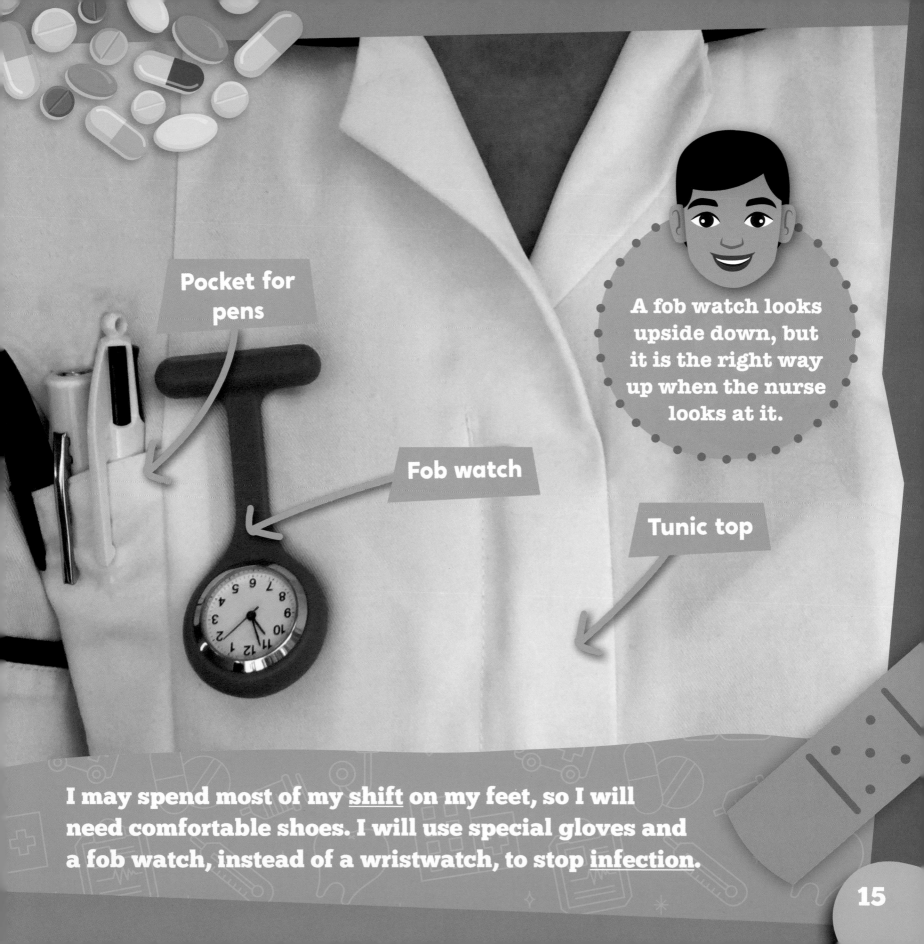

Pocket for pens

Fob watch

Tunic top

A fob watch looks upside down, but it is the right way up when the nurse looks at it.

I may spend most of my <u>shift</u> on my feet, so I will need comfortable shoes. I will use special gloves and a fob watch, instead of a wristwatch, to stop <u>infection</u>.

15

WHAT EQUIPMENT WILL I USE?

Let's have a look at some of the equipment I will use.

Stethoscope – used to hear sounds made by the heart, lungs or tummy

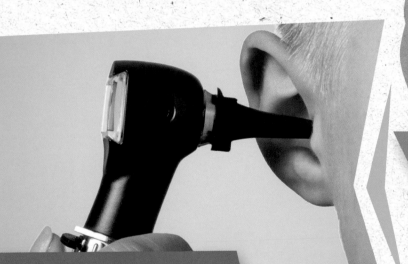

Otoscope – used to look into ears

Blood pressure monitor – used to check how well blood is flowing around the body

16

Thermometer – used to check a patient's temperature

Syringe – used to inject medicine into the body

Bandages and sticking plasters – used to cover injuries

17

WORKING IN THE
COMMUNITY

Lots of nurses work in their local community, visiting patients at home. Health visitors are nurses who visit parents to check that their children are growing up healthily.

Health visitor

This district nurse is applying a new bandage.

If I want to be a health visitor or district nurse, I will have to do extra training.

District nurses care for patients of all ages at home. Often, these patients are elderly or have just come home from hospital. District nurses also teach other family members how to care for the patient.

WHERE COULD I WORK AROUND THE WORLD?

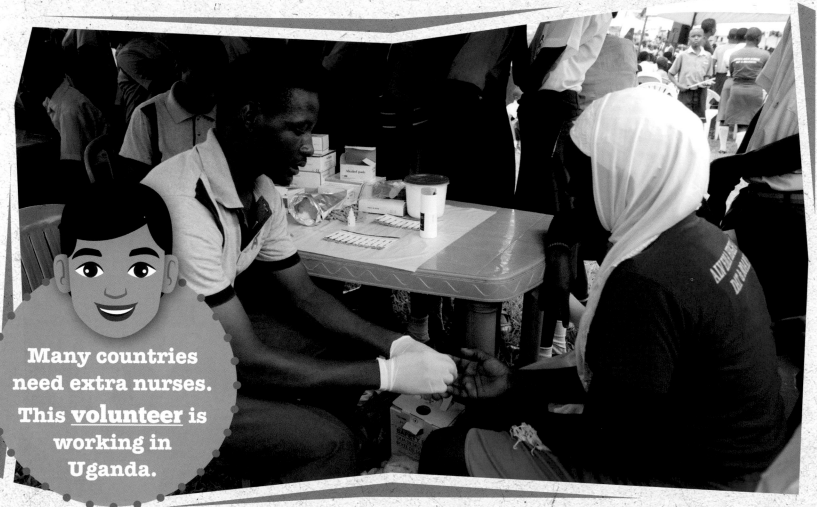

Many countries need extra nurses. This **volunteer** is working in Uganda.

Nurses are needed to give urgent care after natural disasters, such as earthquakes. I might become a volunteer and help people affected by natural disasters, in countries such as India and Nepal.

Some countries are affected by outbreaks of deadly <u>diseases</u>. I might become a volunteer nurse in these countries. Volunteers treat ill people and teach others how to protect themselves and their families from disease.

WHAT DOES A SCHOOL NURSE DO?

They check whether young people have any health conditions and help them to find extra care.

They offer information and advice on health matters, such as head lice.

They see children in their first year at school, to check that they can see and hear properly.

They work with schoolchildren to look after their health and well-being.

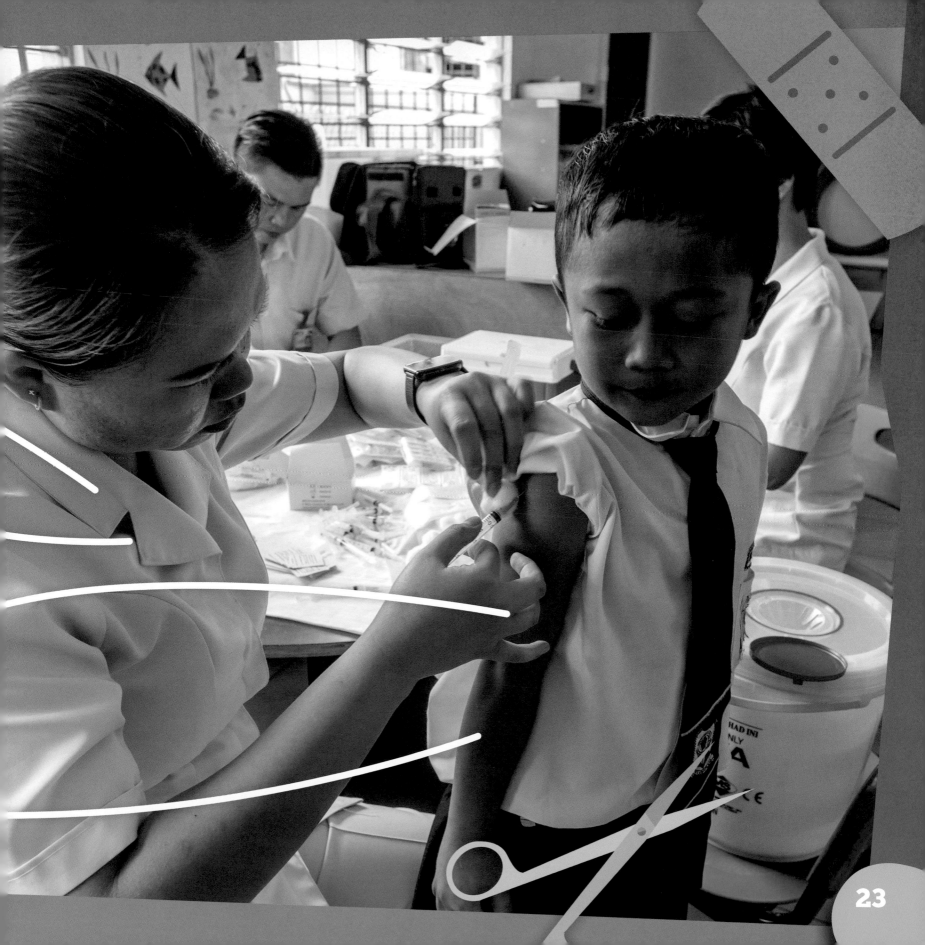

GOSR

ASTHMA	a condition that causes breathing difficulties
BLOOD PRESSURE	how hard and quickly blood is pumped around the body
COMMUNITY	a group of people who live and work together in the same place
DISEASES	illnesses that cause harm to the health of a person
INFECTION	illness caused by dirt or microbes getting into the body
PATIENTS	people who are given medical care or treatment
PRIVACY	the state of being away from the view of other people
SHIFT	the period of time when a person is set to be at work
TEMPERATURE	how cold or hot something or someone is
TREATMENTS	medicine or other types of care that help cure a disease or heal an injury
VOLUNTEER	a person who works or helps others without being paid
WARD	a hospital room with beds for a particular group of patients, such as children

INDEX